New Songs of
Praise 5

The New Songs of Praise series is a resource
for organists, choirmasters, music directors,
clergy and ministers, indeed for all who are
interested in material for congregational
worship. The choice of material is
deliberately wide-ranging and not geared
towards any one sort of liturgical or cultural
pattern.

The procedure for obtaining permission to
copy any item for congregational use is
extremely simple, and is outlined in the
copyright notes.

OXFORD UNIVERSITY PRESS

BBC PUBLICATIONS

1990

Published by
Oxford University Press, Walton Street, Oxford OX2 6DP
Oxford New York Toronto
Delhi Bombay Calcutta Madras Karachi
Petaling Jaya Singapore Hong Kong Tokyo
Nairobi Dar es Salaam Cape Town
Melbourne Auckland
and associated companies in
Beirut Ibadan

Oxford is a trade mark of Oxford University Press

and BBC Publications
A division of BBC Enterprises Ltd
35 Marylebone High Street
London W1M 4AA

© Oxford University Press 1990
First printed 1990

ISBN 0 19 197725 X (OUP)
ISBN 0 563 20895 3 (BBC)

Printed in Great Britain by Information Press, Oxford

CONTENTS

COPYRIGHT

PREFACE

The custom of Christingle (meaning Christ Light) began in the Moravian congregation at Marienborn, Germany, on 20 December 1747, at a children's service conducted by John de Watteville. Christingles were distributed, and the service ended with the prayer, Lord Jesus, kindle a flame in these dear children's hearts, that theirs like Thine become.

The Christingle Service was introduced into the United Kingdom by the Children's Society at Lincoln Cathedral in 1968. With its growing popularity across England and Wales, and with a season of appropriateness extending from Advent to Candlemas, the publication of four Christingle hymns in this collection is most timely.

Today, at the climax of the service each child receives a Christingle which is an orange, representing God's world, in which is mounted a lighted candle representing Christ, the Light of the World. In addition, the orange has four sticks inserted into it on which are impaled nuts, raisins, and sweets. These stand for the created order over which Christ is King, and for God's bounty and goodness to us in providing the fruits of the earth in their season. Finally, a red ribbon surrounds the orange to remind us of the Passion of Christ, through which our salvation has come.

This supplement includes hymns which express the values behind the imagery of Christingle, hymns which convey the stance of deepened spirituality and enhanced wholeness on the part of those receptive to the Light of Christ, and hymns which express the concern and commitment of those strengthened for service by the flame of Christ's love.

This collection will greatly enrich our congregational hymnody, not least in the context of Christingle, and will offer new horizons to a devotional approach.

The Revd. John Bradford
Chaplain Missioner, The Children's Society

1 CHRIST IS GOING TO THE FATHER

EBENEZER (TON-Y-BOTEL) 87 87 D

From an anthem by
Thomas Williams 1869-1944

1. Christ is go - ing to the Fa - ther:

heaven and hell and earth, at - tend!

Marked by blood, in death made per - fect,

see the Man to God as - cend.

Love was＿ cap - tured, cursed and＿ mur - dered:

in the＿ los - ing, love has＿ won;

in the＿ dy - ing, love has＿ ri - sen,

by its＿ ru - in, gained＿ a throne.

Alternative tune: TANYMARIAN

Christ is going to the Father:
heaven and hell and earth, attend!
Marked by blood, in death made perfect,
see the Man to God ascend.
Love was captured, cursed and murdered:
in the losing, love has won;
in the dying, love has risen,
by its ruin, gained a throne.

2 Christ is going to the Father
from the world he came to save,
bringing life to those who listen,
raised in wonder from their grave.
Eldest of a new creation,
Head of all, he leads the way,
calling, drawing us to follow,
sharing his ascension day.

3 Christ is going to the Father:
hear a newborn nation cry –
earth renewed by heaven's music,
Glory be to God on high!
Sing Hosanna, all believers;
Hallelujah, shout his name:
Jesus, universal Saviour,
all the universe proclaim.

Christopher Idle
based on John 16:28

2 A HYMN FOR HEALERS

BUNESSAN 55 54 D

Old Gaelic melody
harmonized by Martin Shaw

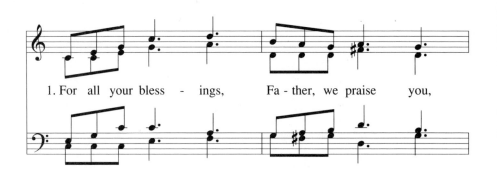

1. For all your bless - ings, Fa - ther, we praise you,

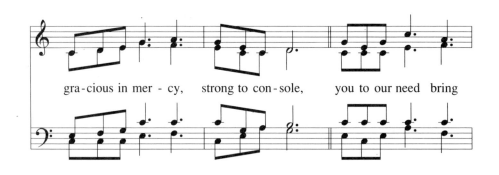

gra - cious in mer - cy, strong to con - sole, you to our need bring

com - fort and heal - ing, love and for - give - ness, ma - king us whole.

For all your blessings, Father, we praise you,
gracious in mercy, strong to console,
you to our need bring comfort and healing,
love and forgiveness, making us whole.

2 Daily around us pain and confusion
crumble our feeble faith into dust.
Yet still we find your love in the darkness,
changing our anxious thoughts into trust.

3 Into your presence we carry with us
prisoners of sickness, sadness and fear;
grant them to know your peace in their suffering
and new life flowing when you are near.

4 Grant to your servants grace to work with you
that in your loving task we may share;
mind's understanding, hands skilled for healing,
hearts of compassion, joined in love's care.

Alan Luff

3 A PRAYER FOR THE NEW DAY

EASTON

Alan Luff

pre - sence in your world, and greet - ing me in all I___

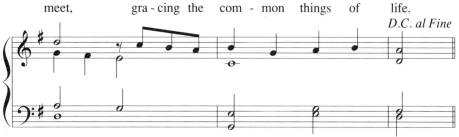

meet, gra - cing the com - mon things of life.

D.C. al Fine

Give us, O God, in this new day
faith putting forth new shoots of hope,
with roots sunk deep into your love –
a day to grow in likeness of Christ.

1 Grant me to find you this new day,
   a hidden presence in your world,
   and greeting me in all I meet,
   gracing the common things of life.
   Give us, O God...

2 Grant me the courage this new day
   to face the pain that round me lies
   the sympathy to share the hurt,
   to know you in the sufferer's eyes.
   Give us, O God...

3 Grant me sincerity this day,
   and openness to all around,
   to know the time when words bring life,
   to know the time when silence heals.

   So, when this day draws to its close,
   may we with all God's people know
   Love's breadth and length and height and depth –
   that we have grown in likeness of Christ.

Alan Luff
after Ephesians 3:17-18

4 COME, SPIRIT, COME!

EAST ACKLAM 8484 8884

Francis Jackson

1. Gift of Christ from __ God __ our Fa - ther, Come, Spi - rit, come! ___ Well of life, and gene - rous Gi - ver, Come, __ Spi - rit, come! ___ With Your light our minds en - light - en, With Your grace our ta - lents height - en,

Alternative tune: AR HYD Y NOS

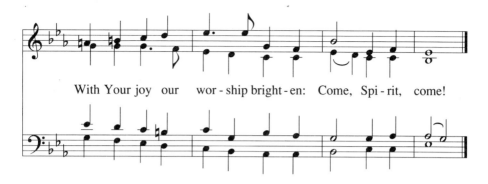

With Your joy our wor-ship bright-en: Come, Spi-rit, come!

Gift of Christ from God our Father,
    Come, Spirit, come!
Well of life and generous Giver,
    Come, Spirit, come!
With your light our minds enlighten,
With Your grace our talents heighten,
With Your joy our worship brighten:
    Come, Spirit, come!

2 Gift of Christ to guide and teach us,
    Come, Spirit, come!
Counsellor so swift to reach us,
    Come, Spirit, come!
Christ is Lord, so may we name Him:
Never fearfully disclaim Him
But to all the world proclaim Him.
    Come, Spirit, come!

3 Gift of Christ to help us praying,
    Come, Spirit, come!
Advocate beside us staying,
    Come, Spirit, come!
In the work of intercession,
In the healing of confession,
In success and in depression,
    Come, Spirit, come!

4 Gift of Christ for our salvation,
    Come, Spirit, come!
Bring to birth Your new creation,
    Come, Spirit, come!
All the devil's work undoing,
Christ's own ministry pursuing,
Glory in the Church renewing!
    Come, Spirit, come!

David Mowbray

5 DESTINY

INNSBRUCK 776 778

Traditional song set by H. Isaac *c.*1450–1527
Harmony by J. S. Bach 1685–1750

1. Lord, in my life's un - fold - ing I

can and will ac - know - ledge Your o - ver - arch - ing care. From

in - fan - cy and school - age, Sus - tain - ing, gui - ding,

hold - ing, A deep - er force than chance was there.

Lord, in my life's unfolding
I can and will acknowledge
    Your over-arching care.
From infancy and school-age,
Sustaining, guiding, holding,
    A deeper force than chance was there.

2 No voice from heaven dictated
The course that I decided,
    No pointing finger showed.
But where the paths divided
In love you stood and waited
    To guide my steps on either road.

3 My destiny is charted,
But every passing second
    The chart is drawn anew;
The course in heaven reckoned
Is reappraised, re-started,
    To take account of what I do.

4 So will I praise the patience
Which, times beyond recalling,
    Has seen and understood;
Which saved my feet from falling,
And used my inclinations
    To make another kind of good.

Michael Hewlett

6 HOW LONG, O LORD, HOW LONG?

HARRELL

Sue Mitchell Wallace

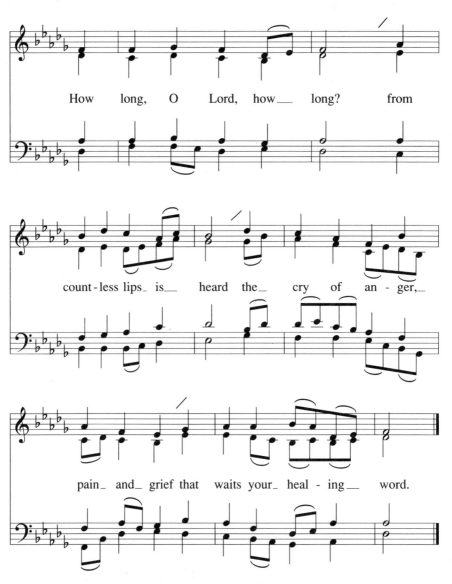

How long, O Lord, how_ long? from count-less lips_ is_ heard the_ cry of an - ger,_ pain_ and_ grief that waits your_ heal - ing_ word.

The tune, when sent to me by the composer, called to mind the refrain of Harrell Beck's Lecture on the Psalms of Lament that he gave to the Hymn Society of America and this immediately formed the first line of this Hymn of Lament. The composer and I both agreed to call the tune HARRELL, and we dedicate the hymn to his memory. *Alan Luff*

Alternative tune: SOUTHWELL

How long, O Lord, how long?
from countless lips is heard
the cry of anger, pain and grief
that waits your healing word.

2   They wait your healing word
who in their anguish grope
for answers to life's mystery,
and look to you for hope.

3   They look to you for hope:
and find, to share their loss,
the God who as a suffering man
still hangs upon a cross.

4   You hang upon the cross
to show us that the way
still leads through pain if we would reach
the resurrection day.

Alan Luff

7 BRING YOUR CHRISTINGLE

Valerie Ruddle

Bring your Christ - in - gle with glad - ness and joy! Sing

praise to God who gave us his Son; So give Him,

give Him your love. Here is an or - ange —

Verse – repeat as necessary

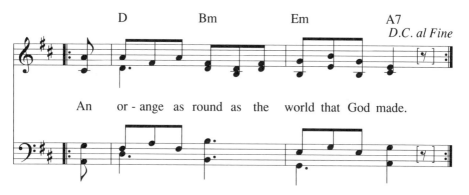

An or - ange as round as the world that God made.

Bring your Christingle with gladness and joy!
Sing praise to God who gave us his Son;
So give Him, give Him your love.

(Leader)   Here is an orange –

(All)   An orange as round as the world that God made.

2   *(Leader)*   Here is a candle –

   (All)   A candle for Jesus, the Light of the world,
     An orange as round as the world that God made;

3   *(Leader)*   Here is red ribbon –

   (All)   Red ribbon reminds us Christ died for us all;
     A candle for Jesus, the Light of the world;
     An orange as round as the world that God made;

4   *(Leader)*   Here as the fruits –

   (All)   The fruits of the earth God has given us to share;
     Red ribbon reminds us Christ died for us all;
     A candle for Jesus, the Light of the world;
     An orange as round as the world that God made;

Valerie Ruddle and William Horton

8 CHRISTINGLE CAROL

Traditional English

It's rounded like an orange,
  this earth on which we stand;
and we praise the God who holds it
  in the hollow of his hand.
  So Father, we would thank you
    for all that you have done,
  and for all that you have given us
    through the coming of your Son.

2 A candle, burning brightly,
    can cheer the darkest night
  and these candles tell how Jesus
    came to bring a dark world light.

3 The ribbon round the orange
    reminds us of the cost;
  how the Shepherd, strong and gentle,
    gave his life to save the lost.

4 Four seasons with their harvest
    supply the food we need,
  and the Spirit gives a harvest
    that can make us rich indeed.

5 We come with our Christingles
    to tell of Jesus' birth
  and we praise the God who blessed us
    by his coming to this earth.

Basil Bridge

9 GOD WHOSE LOVE IS EVERYWHERE

FALLING FIFTHS 7775 775

Noël Tredinnick

Gm/E   A⁷   Dm   Optional link

praise   the   God   of   love!

leader (handwritten)   *Cong.* (handwritten)

The orange,
representing
all the world

God whose love is everywhere
made our earth and all things fair,
ever keeps them in his care;
    praise the God of love!
He who hung the stars in space
holds the spinning world in place;
    praise the God of love!

leader (handwritten)   *Cong* (handwritten)

The sticks,
fruit and nuts,
representing
the four
seasons and
the fruit of
the earth

2 Come with thankful songs to sing
of the gifts the seasons bring,
summer, winter, autumn, spring;
    praise the God of love!
He who gave us breath and birth
gives us all the fruitful earth;
    praise the God of love!

leader (handwritten)   *Cong* (handwritten)

The red
ribbon,
representing
the blood of
Christ shed
for us

3 Mark what love the Lord displayed,
all our sins upon him laid,
by his blood our ransom paid;
    praise the God of love!
Circled by that scarlet band
all the world is in his hand;
    praise the God of love!

leader (handwritten)   *Cong* (handwritten)

The lighted
candle,
representing
Christ
the Light of
the world

4 See the sign of love appear,
flame of glory, bright and clear,
light for all the world is here;
    praise the God of love!
Gloom and darkness, get you gone!
Christ the Light of life has shone;
    praise the God of love!

Timothy Dudley-Smith

10 NOW WE HOLD THE RIPENED ORANGE

CALON LAN 8787D

John Hughes (1872-1914)

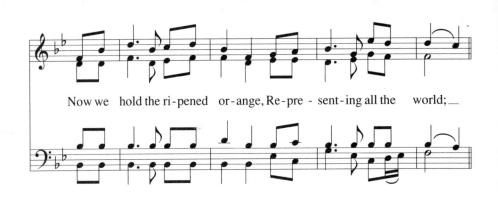

Now we hold the ri-pened or-ange, Re-pre - sent-ing all the world; ___

Cir-cled by a crim-son rib-bon As the sym-bol of Christ's blood.

Let God's gra-cious way of lo - ving Bring his joy to ev-ery place,

As his glo-rious light for li-ving Bright-ly gleams on ev - ery face.

Alternative tune: CONVERSE ('What a friend we have in Jesus')

A family hymn for Christingle celebrations, after the candles are lit

Now we hold the ripened orange,
Representing all the world;
Circled by a crimson ribbon
As the symbol of Christ's blood.
Let God's gracious way of loving
Bring his joy to every place,
As his glorious light for living
Brightly gleams on every face.

2 Let the sticks of food remind us,
By the word of God revealed,
That each cycle of the seasons
Will its fruitful harvest yield.

3 By our pleasure at life's goodness,
Which the nuts and fruit suggest,
May we learn to right injustice:
So may everyone be blessed.

4 May the light of countless candles,
Bravely burning everywhere,
Help us all to follow Jesus
Through a life of faith and care.

Peter Dewdney